Jason Glaser

CONTENTS

Rigby

A Harcourt Achieve Imprint

www.Rigby.com

1-800-531-5015

Beginning to Tell Time

Even thousands of years ago, people saw that the earth experienced cycles like the ones we see today. They saw the sun and moon rise and set in the sky. They felt the temperature drop as the sun slipped below the **horizon**. They learned that the rain would turn to snow as the days got shorter and colder.

The sun has just come up over the horizon to indicate the start of a new day.

Early **astronomers** tracked the length of a year by watching the cycle of the sun's path in the sky. They counted the days it took to complete a cycle and start back at the beginning. This cycle of the sun became a year.

People who lived thousands of years ago next organized time into smaller units by tracking changes in the moon. The number of days from one full moon to the next became a month.

Early Egyptian tablets from 3000 B.C. showed that people also divided the day into units. This helped early cultures determine how many hours of daylight to expect. Knowing how many hours of daylight they had at different times of the year helped farmers know when to work their land.

New Moon   First Quarter Moon   Full Moon   Third Quarter Moon

Before Calendars and Clocks

Eventually, people began to use tools to mark time more precisely. The simplest tool was called a *gnomon* (NO-mun). A gnomon was simply a stick or pole stuck into the ground. The length and direction of the pole's shadow showed the time of day or year.

A sundial is a kind of gnomon. It gives the general time of day by casting a shadow onto a circle that is marked off in hours. Sundials were used widely for many centuries and are still used today, although they are used mostly for decoration.

Sundials and the giant-sized stones of Stonehenge were used to tell time long before people invented clocks.

Perhaps one of the most famous timekeeping tools is Stonehenge, built in England in prehistoric times. Stonehenge is a circle of carefully placed gigantic stones. No one really knows exactly what Stonehenge was used for, but it is believed that the shadows cast by the sun show the shortest and longest days of the year and tell when a month has passed.

The Need to Tell Time

The most important reason for tracking the time of year was so farmers could know when to plant crops. By counting the months from the middle of winter or by measuring the amount of daylight, farmers could predetermine when to plant and when to harvest. People could save enough food to last the winter if they understood the seasonal cycle.

The word *season* comes from the Latin word for **sowing**. Over time, season has come to mean any period of similar, **predictable** weather patterns. The seasons we all recognize in a year include spring, summer, autumn, and winter. Each has its own weather pattern. The weather patterns that create the seasons are due to the movements of the earth around the sun. Because the sun affects opposite sides of the earth differently, two seasons occur at the same time on Earth. When it is cold winter in the United States, it is warm summer in Australia.

spr

sum

autu

wir

Each season is caused by Earth's spinning around as it moves on its path around the sun.

② Earth Goes 'Round, Seasons Go 'Round

The story of the seasons really begins with the sun, the source of all life on the earth. The sun provides energy in the form of rays that strike Earth, heat it, and provide enough warmth to support the plants and animals living there. However, the sun's rays fall on Earth unevenly, and this causes some parts of the planet to be warmer than others.

Did you know the temperature on the outside of the sun is about 11,000°F?

7

The Round Earth

Why don't all places on Earth receive the same amount of sunlight? The main reason is Earth's **spherical** shape. Although the planet receives sunlight over a wide area, its edges do not receive as much direct sunlight as its center. The sun appears high in the sky and is very bright to those people who are close to Earth's center. People further from that point will see the sun lower in the sky. The same thing happens as the day begins and the sun moves up over the horizon. The rays grow stronger until noon when the sun is at its highest point of the day. As afternoon moves on, the sun sinks down and Earth grows cooler again.

These dolphins are making playful leaps in the air as the sun sets on another day.

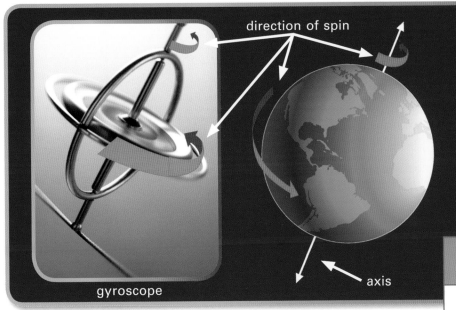

direction of spin

gyroscope

axis

Beating Time

If you flew directly from Sydney, Australia, to Los Angeles, California, you would seem to land before you took off. This is because the sun rises in Sydney 18 hours before it does in Los Angeles and the flight takes 14 hours.

Our Spinning Earth

Earth spins around an invisible line called an **axis**. Earth is always spinning, so the part of Earth facing the sun is always changing. Because of this **rotation**, the sun appears to move across the sky. But it is really Earth that is turning.

Earth spins toward the east on its axis, which causes the sun to seem to rise up out of the east and set in the west. This is also the reason why sunrise occurs earlier the farther you travel to the east.

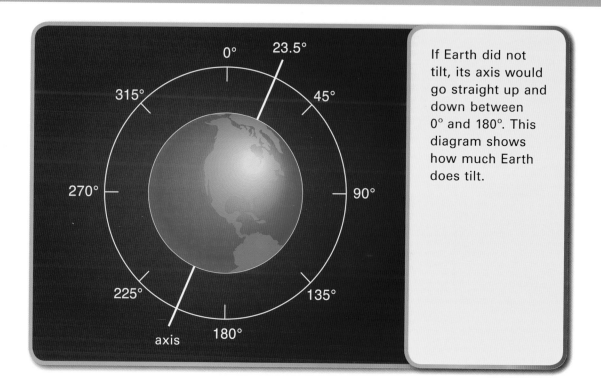

If Earth did not tilt, its axis would go straight up and down between 0° and 180°. This diagram shows how much Earth does tilt.

It takes Earth 24 hours to complete a single rotation. When part of Earth faces the sun, it is daytime, and when it faces away, it is nighttime. If Earth were to spin like a basketball on the tip of a finger, without leaning or wobbling, every place on the planet except the North and South Poles would receive 12 hours of light and 12 hours of darkness every day. However, Earth is tilted on its axis at 23.5 **degrees** (23.5°). This causes some parts of the planet to receive more light each day than other parts.

Our Revolving Earth

Earth moves in ways other than rotating. You may have noticed that the sun shines for a longer time in the summer and a shorter time in the winter. This is because of the way Earth tilts as it moves around the sun. One trip around the sun is called a **revolution**. One revolution takes a little more than 365 days to complete. That equals one year.

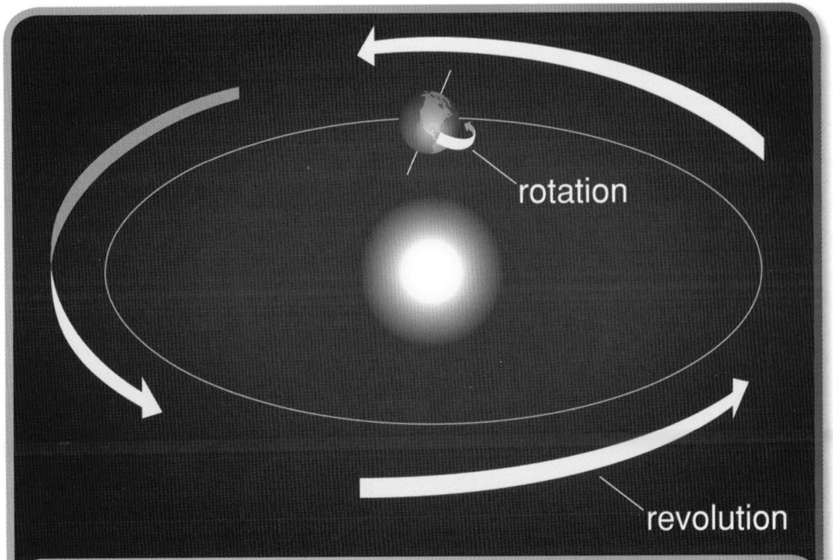

Most of the world uses the same calendar, named the Gregorian calendar. This calendar begins each new year at midnight on January 1. The year ends at midnight on the following December 31. February has 28 days most of the time. However, every fourth year February has 29 days. These years are called "leap years" and allow the calendar and sun to catch up with each other. It takes Earth almost 6 hours longer than 365 days to go around the sun. Four of these extra 6 hours equals the extra 24-hour day in a leap year.

rotation

revolution

The diagram shows how Earth travels around the sun. The small arrow shows how Earth spins. The bigger arrows show Earth's revolution around the sun. Earth makes a complete revolution around the sun in 365 days.

Earth's revolution around the sun is a slightly oval–shaped path called an **ellipse**. Because the path of Earth's revolution is an oval, Earth is slightly closer to the sun for half the year. Many people think that the hottest seasons happen when Earth is closest to the sun, but this is not true. Being closer to the sun does add a small amount of heat to Earth. However, it is the angle of the sun's rays as they hit Earth that determines the seasons.

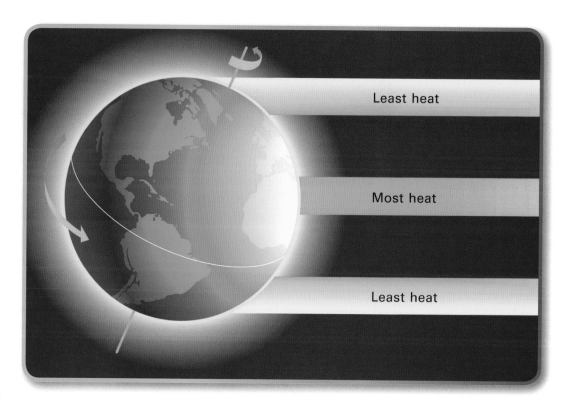

③ Measuring Time and Distance on Earth

Lines of Latitude and Longitude

The earliest mapmakers wanted to draw imaginary lines around Earth to help make their maps. They decided to use the center, which is the fattest part of Earth, as the starting point and the two poles at either end of Earth as end points. Beginning with the center, which is called the equator, they drew lines at equal distances from each other going around the earth. These lines are called lines of latitude.

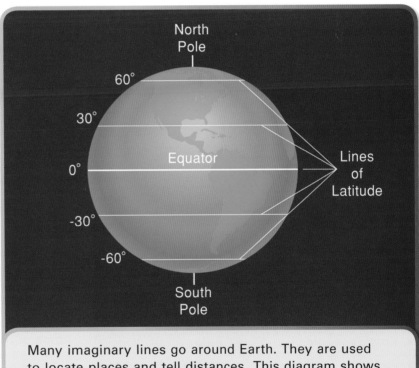

Many imaginary lines go around Earth. They are used to locate places and tell distances. This diagram shows a few of these lines of latitude.

A circle is divided into 360°, or 360 degrees. So is Earth. A total of 360 imaginary lines go from the North Pole to the South Pole. These are lines of longitude. They are used to find distances and locations, as are the lines of latitude.

Lines of longitude start at 0° and go east and west up to 180°. Longitude lines on the east side of 0° end in E, as in 170° E. Western longitude lines end in W, as in 160° W.

Longitude and Latitude

To help you remember which lines are longitude and which are latitude, think of a clue. For example, *lat* means *side*. This can help you remember that latitude lines go from side to side, or east to west. *Longitude* starts with *long*, which can help you remember that these long lines go up and down.

North Pole

-60° -30° 0° 30° 60°

Lines of Longitude

Prime Meridian

South Pole

Lines of longitude start at 0° (degrees) and continue to the east and west of the center line of longitude, at 0°, which is known as the Prime Meridian. The Prime Meridian passes through Greenwich, England, which is the home of the Royal Observatory. The decision to use this as the 0° line was made in 1884.

Lines of longitude are also useful when it comes to telling time. The Prime Meridian is at 0°. Halfway around the globe, at about 180°, is the International Date Line, which runs mostly through the Pacific Ocean. This is where each new day on Earth begins. As you move from date line to date line, you can see how time changes. If you travel to the east, each time zone adds one hour to the day. Therefore, when it is 12:00 P.M. in Chicago, it is 1:00 P.M. in New York, which is one time zone to the east of Chicago. When you travel west, it is one hour earlier for each time zone you go through. If it is 5:00 P.M. in Chicago and you are two time zones west in San Francisco, the time in San Francisco is two hours earlier, making it 3:00 P.M.

Each new day on Earth begins at 12:00 A.M. at the International Date Line. Pretend the date has just turned to October 1 at the Date Line. If you called someone in the first time zone to the west, at that person's house it would still be September 30 at 11:00 P.M. If you called someone in the first time zone to the east, it would be 11:00 A.M. on September 30. The people to the west would be one hour behind your time, but the people to the east would be 23 hours behind. That could get quite confusing!

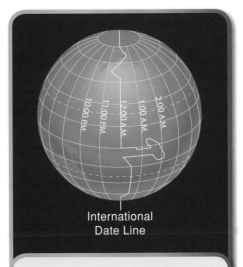

International
Date Line

The International Date Line was drawn so that most of it is over water. That helps make some of the time differences less of a problem. Notice that the Date Line is not straight. It zigzags a bit so the islands in the area will all be on the same time and date. Several other date lines are also not straight, especially if they split a smaller state or country that wants all of its people to be in the same time zone.

Hemisphere

The equator divides the earth into the Northern and Southern **Hemispheres**. The Northern Hemisphere contains all of North America, Europe, and Asia. It also has a small part of Africa and some of South America. The Southern Hemisphere contains Australia, Antarctica, and most of Africa and South America.

The sun's rays strike the equator more directly than they strike most of the earth. Therefore, places near the equator tend to be warm or hot year 'round. Places at the poles tend to be much colder.

This view looks up at the South Pole, which is at the bottom of Earth. It shows part of the Southern Hemisphere. Can you find the tip of South America?

This view of Earth looks down on the North Pole, which is at the top of the earth. It shows part of the Northern Hemisphere. Can you find where you live?

This globe is looking at the earth from the side, so you can see part of the Northern Hemisphere and part of the Southern Hemisphere.

Earth continues to rotate as it travels on its yearlong trip. In each revolution around the sun, Earth reaches a point where one tip of the axis is leaning toward the sun and one tip of the axis is leaning away. The hemisphere leaning toward the sun receives more sunlight. The hemisphere leaning away from the sun receives less sunlight.

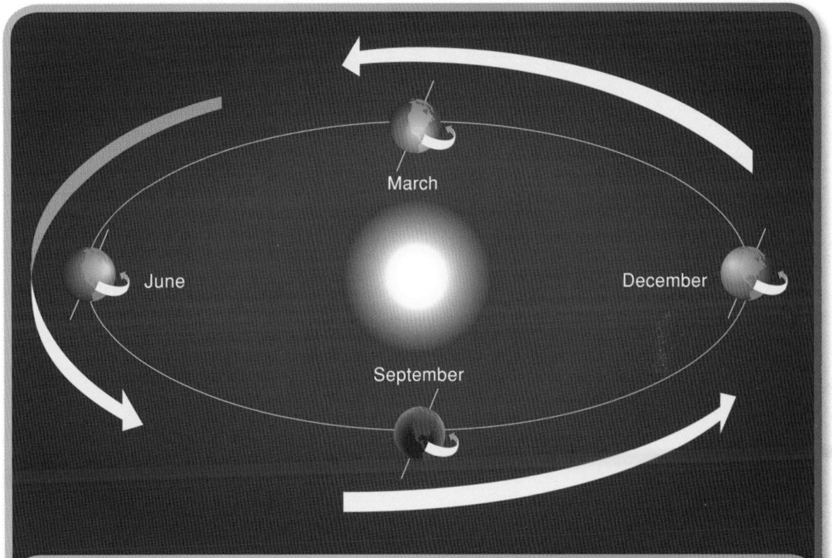

North America is in the top, or Northern, Hemisphere. Look at the North Pole in June. It is tilting toward the sun. This means the rest of the Northern Hemisphere is also tilting toward the sun in June, causing it to be summer. The North Pole is tilting away from the sun in December, causing the season of winter in the Northern Hemisphere.

The diagram shows Earth at four places on its trip around the sun. Notice how Earth always tilts in the same direction. This causes the sun's rays to shine on different areas as Earth makes its revolution each year.

Earth is still tilting in March and September, but the tilt is sideways to the sun. Neither of Earth's poles is pointing toward the sun or away from it. They are just pointing to the side. On two days of the year, one in March and the other in September, each day is 12 hours long and each night is 12 hours long.

17

Equinoxes and Solstices

What would happen if we had only one hour of daylight each day? We have become used to working, eating, and staying active while the sun is out to keep us warm and help us see. Plants would not grow as big, and we would need to light our homes all day. What other changes might we see?

Many early cultures divided the year into four seasons, based on the length of the day compared to the length of the night. They studied carefully the movements of the sun and moon through the sky. And they marked the beginning of each season with a special celebration.

WHEN DO THE SEASONS BEGIN?

	NORTHERN HEMISPHERE	SOUTHERN HEMISPHERE
Spring (vernal equinox)	March 20	September 22
Summer (summer solstice)	June 21	December 21
Fall (autumnal equinox)	September 22	March 20
Winter (winter solstice)	December 21	June 21

(These dates may change by a day or two each year.)

Today, we know much more about how and why the seasons change. Satellites, spacecraft, and huge telescopes constantly provide images for scientists to study. Using all of that information, we still recognize the same four seasons, and the beginning of each season is marked by a special event in the sky. It is amazing how well early cultures understood the seasons, even without the scientific tools used today. This shows how important seasons and their connection to the weather have been throughout history.

Equinox and Solstice

Four events in the sky mark the beginning of each season. Two are equinoxes, and two are solstices.

An equinox is a day when light and dark are equally long. On the days of the two equinoxes, every place on Earth has a 12-hour day and a 12-hour night. Earth's axis is tilting sideways to the sun, not toward the sun or away from it. The vernal equinox marks the first day of spring, and the autumnal equinox marks the first day of autumn, or fall.

A solstice occurs when Earth's axis is either pointing as far as it can toward the sun or away from the sun. When Earth's axis at the North Pole is pointing toward the sun during the summer solstice, it makes our part of Earth warmer. The winter solstice is when the axis at the North Pole points away from the sun and our part of Earth becomes colder.

Seasonal Myth

A common legend says that on the day of the vernal equinox, you can stand an egg on one end. Every year, people try to balance eggs on this day, and it usually works! What people may not know is that you can do this at any time—with the right egg. Eggs often have bumps on one end that help them remain balanced. The seasons have nothing to do with it!

Long ago, equinoxes and solstices helped people prepare for shifts in the climate. The vernal equinox meant that the coming days would be getting longer. People would have more daylight than night. This was a time to start planting. The summer solstice meant that the day would still be longer than the night, but each day would be shorter than the day before. This indicated that the planting season would be ending soon. The autumnal equinox, when day and night were each 12 hours, let people know that the days would keep getting shorter, and there would be more dark hours than light hours. It was time to harvest the crops and start storing food and fuel for winter. Finally, the winter solstice, the shortest day of the year, found everyone boarded up in their shelters, waiting for spring to reappear.

By following the changes in daylight and dark, people knew when to plant their crops and when to harvest them.

About 90 percent of Earth's population lives in the Northern Hemisphere. The dates for each equinox and solstice are based on the Northern Hemisphere seasons. For example, the equinox that begins the Northern spring is the vernal (green, or spring) equinox. The summer solstice, autumnal equinox, and winter solstice also name the seasons in the Northern Hemisphere. These solstices and equinoxes occur in the Southern Hemisphere, but they are exactly opposite. When it's winter in the Northern Hemisphere, it's summer in the Southern Hemisphere. When it's spring in the United States, it's fall in Brazil.

March 20: beginning of spring in the Northern Hemisphere

March 20: beginning of fall in the Southern Hemisphere

Celebrations

Many cultures across the world today celebrate the equinoxes and solstices as they did in the past. Harvest celebrations around the globe include dancing, singing, and, of course, feasting on the harvested food. In addition,

- **Japan** celebrates the vernal equinox by reading poetry and enjoying the new spring blossoms.

- **Sweden** celebrates the summer solstice by singing, eating with friends, and dancing around a *Majstang*, or maypole.

- **China** celebrates *Dong Zhi* (The Extreme of Winter) by sharing meals and celebrating the return of longer daylight.

Effects on Global Temperature

Between the spring equinox and the summer solstice, the Northern Hemisphere gets more direct sun than at any other time of the year. This causes the temperature in the Northern Hemisphere to rise. During this time, the sun seems to climb higher in the sky during the day and stay up longer as well. The day of the summer solstice, when the sun is highest, is the longest day of the year.

After the summer solstice, the days get shorter, but the weather stays warm. If you wonder why this happens, think of a pot on a stove. Once you remove the pot from the flame, the pot stays warm for a while. The earth's **atmosphere** and oceans hold heat from the sun in the same way.

This heat energy stays around after the sun's rays have passed. In the Northern Hemisphere, the longest days are in June. However, the earth will stay very warm through July and August. It will only cool down once the days are shorter than the nights.

These people are exercising, playing, or working in the hot summer sun.

The shortest days happen and the smallest amount of sun energy is received by Earth on the winter solstice. However, remember that the atmosphere still holds onto some of the sun's energy and heat. The coldest days of winter arrive only after the last of this energy has escaped Earth's atmosphere. In the Northern Hemisphere, this usually happens in January and February.

The shortest day of the year is in December, but often the coldest days don't come until January or February.

When winter does arrive, people find many different ways to enjoy it.

The Flip Side

One end of Earth's axis leans toward the sun during a solstice, and the other end of the axis leans away. Because of this, the two hemispheres have opposite seasons at the same time of the calendar year. As the sun beats down on the Northern Hemisphere in June and July to cause summer, the days are shorter in the Southern Hemisphere. Below the equator, June and July are winter months. In December and January, the Southern Hemisphere enjoys the summer, while winter weather chills the Northern Hemisphere.

This is Sydney in January, the warmest month of the year in Australia. Many people in the United States could not go to the beach in January because of the cold winter weather.

This difference between how cold winter gets in some parts of the world and how warm it stays in other parts is partly due to the oceans. Oceans, like the atmosphere, work as an **insulator**, keeping heat in the earth. Much of the Southern Hemisphere is water. The oceans trap heat during the summer and release it slowly during the winter. This helps keep Australia, Africa, and South America from becoming extremely cold in the winter because they are surrounded by so much water.

This is Sydney in July, the coldest month of the year in Australia. Think about what the temperature is like in July where you live.

5 The Four Seasons in Detail

We know that people living in the Northern Hemisphere are the ones who named the equinoxes. But where did the season's names come from? To find out, we must travel back hundreds of years.

The names of the seasons developed from many different cultures. Notice that all the names describe natural events that occur during many of the seasons.

Where do the names of the seasons come from?

SPRING			SUMMER		
Word	Origin	Meaning	Word	Origin	Meaning
spring	Old English	rise up	sumar	German	season
AUTUMN			WINTER		
Word	Origin	Meaning	Word	Origin	Meaning
autumnus	Latin	fall or descent	wintrus	Old English	Either wet or white

Spring

Springtime is perhaps the most important part of the entire cycle of seasons in nature. Once the ground thaws and plants are no longer in danger of freezing, farmers and gardeners begin planting. As the sun gets higher in the sky, the additional direct sunlight increases the amount of energy for the growing plants and crops. They reproduce and start to sprout and grow. The spring rains, which result from winds shifting from the oceans, further help plants come to life.

Animals also respond to the changes brought about by spring. Many animals give birth in springtime because water and food are more available. They also use the longer days to find or hunt food for their young.

Farms in spring are often home to many baby animals.

Summer

By the time the summer solstice occurs, plants have hopefully received enough rain to be strong enough to withstand the sunlight streaming down over the long summer days. Plants and crops planted too late in spring or early summer might be too small and wither in the hot summer sun.

With plenty of sun and water, the planted crops have enough energy to produce fruits and seeds to help them reproduce. These fruits and seeds, as well as grains, can also be used for food. After the summer solstice, as the days grow shorter, plants absorb less sunlight and water. At this point, many crops are ready for harvest.

Animals, too, thrive during the summer months. If spring has been favorable, there is plenty of food and water. Toward the end of summer, many animals begin to store food for the winter, or eat more oil and fat for those winter days when they can't find food.

This corn looks green and healthy from getting enough water and sunlight.

Fall

After the autumnal equinox, the days get shorter, and the temperatures begin to drop. Farmers sometimes call autumn the "harvest season" because they know that they must harvest their crops before the plants stop producing fruit, seeds, or grains. The danger of crops freezing becomes more likely.

The decrease in sunlight during the fall is a signal to leafy plants that their growing season will soon be over. Many plants' leaves turn brown or drop off–a sign that their need for energy has lowered. Many plants store energy in their roots and enter a time of **dormancy**. That means they won't produce leaves or absorb sunlight again until the next spring. In other words, the plants go to sleep until spring returns.

Animals also begin to prepare for the onset of winter. Some animals begin to **migrate**, or move to warmer places. Others prepare spaces to live, or **hibernate**, in during the winter.

Many people travel long distances to see fall's beautiful colors.

Winter

Winter has a powerful effect on the land as plants die from cold and lack of sunlight. The animals that eat those plants sometimes change their eating habits or move to warmer areas.

Scientists know that the change in the length of the day sends a signal to animals that winter is approaching. Many birds migrate as winter nears in the Northern Hemisphere. They travel at night and follow the changing winds that guide them south toward warmer climates.

Many birds do not migrate but remain and adapt, or make changes, to live through the cold winter. One of these is the white tailed ptarmigan that becomes totally white in winter. Weasels and rabbits grow thicker, white fur. Mice build tunnels through the snow, and squirrels huddle close together.

This flock of geese has left its home in the north and is flying to its winter home farther south. It will return north when the temperatures there begin to warm up.

Animals that don't migrate may hibernate during the winter. Having stored food in the summer and fall, chipmunks begin a period of deep sleep when winter comes and food sources are hard to find. Bears also hibernate and live on the extra fat they added to their bodies before winter arrived. These animals become active again in the spring when plants begin to grow and animals return from their migration.

These animals are hibernating through the winter season. They will become active again when spring arrives.

Humans and the Seasons

Sunlight is just as important to humans as it is to plants and animals. People's bodies respond to the patterns of nature. Certain systems in the body help people know when it is time to sleep at night and wake in the day. The shorter days of winter make some people feel tired. Other people feel sad when they do not get enough sunlight. Sometimes it helps to use special lamps that give off light that is similar to the sun's light.

We know that doctors don't want us to get too much sunlight because it can damage us, but they do want us to get some sunlight every day. When our bodies get sunlight, they make Vitamin D, which is the only vitamin our bodies make naturally. In the summer, 10 to 15 minutes of sunshine a day is enough to make sure our bodies produce vitamin D. During the winter, we may need slightly more time in the sun.

Some people use a special light for a few minutes every day to help them feel better during a long, dark winter.

⑥ Unusual Seasons

     Since seasons depend on the angle at which the sun's rays strike Earth, it should be no surprise that extreme angles can produce some extreme seasons. Some of these extreme seasons occur in the tropics, which is the area on either side of the equator.

     The tropics are marked by two important lines. These lines are named the Tropic of Cancer and the Tropic of Capricorn after two constellations in the sky: Cancer the Crab and Capricorn the Goat. The Tropic of Cancer is a line 23.5° above the equator, and the Tropic of Capricorn is a line 23.5° below the equator.

The area between the Tropic of Cancer and the Tropic of Capricorn is the only area on Earth where the sun ever shines from directly overhead. Having that much sunshine makes this part of Earth very warm and wet. In the tropics, the average temperature is above 64.4° Fahrenheit–for all 12 months!

Tropic of Cancer

Equator

Tropic of Capricorn

Earth's Axis

You can see that the sun is shining directly on the Tropic of Cancer. Remember, the sun isn't moving, but Earth is. The revolution of Earth around the sun causes the direct sunshine to move from one part of the tropics to another.

Monsoon Season

The tropics don't get cold enough to experience the usual four seasons. Instead, tropical seasons are often simply called wet or dry. Many of the wet seasons are caused by monsoon winds that change direction for part of the year and blow from the ocean over the land.

From April to September, the area between the equator and the Tropic of Cancer experiences a wet, rainy season. Meanwhile, the area south of the equator to the Tropic of Capricorn is left with little rain, and has a long dry season. From October to March, the seasons reverse as the sun crosses south of the equator.

The monsoon season usually lasts for several months. Beginning in May, the sun's energy heats the land, and the land's temperature gets hotter than the oceans around it. The cooler air over the oceans pushes in over the land, bringing lots of water with it.

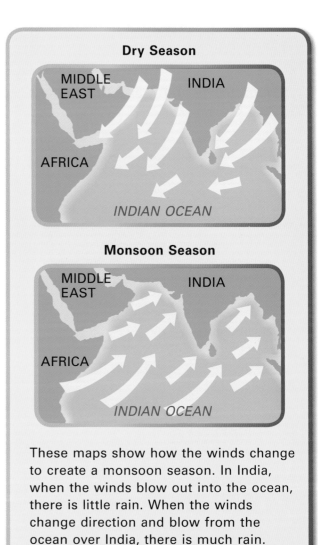

These maps show how the winds change to create a monsoon season. In India, when the winds blow out into the ocean, there is little rain. When the winds change direction and blow from the ocean over India, there is much rain.

The rains brought in by the monsoon winds usually make up most of the rainfall in an area for the entire year. It is possible for 30 to 40 inches of rain to fall in a single day. The rainfall for a season can equal 50 to 70 inches or more. On many occasions, too much rainfall has brought widespread flooding and caused great damage. The flooding is met with mixed feelings. On the one hand, there is sadness at the losses caused by the floods. But on the other hand, the floods provide water for drinking, irrigating crops, and generating electricity.

While the monsoon season brings rain needed in the rice fields and elsewhere, it can also bring flooding. When there is minor flooding, people often go about their normal lives.

Like spring in America, the monsoon's timing is crucial for farmers in the tropics, many of whom grow rice. Rice is grown in paddies, or fields of standing water. So much rain can fall during the monsoon season that it fills fields with water that remains for months.

The wet season is the only chance many places have to grow crops. If farmers wait too long before planting, they can miss the wet weather.

Farmers in the tropics depend on a wet monsoon season for good crops.

Dry Season

Because direct sunlight moves up as far as the Tropic of Cancer and down as far as the Tropic of Capricorn, the sun must pass over the equator twice. It passes over once on its way up to the Tropic of Cancer, and it passes over a second time on its way back down south. This means that the equator actually has two rainy seasons.

After the monsoon season, the winds turn around and push out toward the ocean. This creates a very dry season over the land that lasts for most of the year. Usually, however, so much rain has come down during the rainy season that the land does well during the dry season. In fact, scientists are discovering that the rain forests in the tropics experience their greatest growth during this dry period.

Although the tropics are dry for many months at a time, the monsoon winds bring in enough rain to keep the rain forests healthy all year long.

Hurricane Season

Hurricane season is very dangerous. Hurricanes start as thunderstorms on the land, then move out over the warm ocean water found in the tropics. The warm water helps the storm grow into what is called "a tropical storm." If the tropical storm continues to grow and pick up wind speed, it can become powerful enough to turn into a hurricane.

This photograph was taken by a hurricane research airplane. It shows the eye of Hurricane Elena.

In the Northern Hemisphere, the hurricane season usually begins sometime in June and continues into November. The ocean water, heated by the sun, lifts warm tropical water into the air where it forms into a funnel of swirling winds. This storm system brings high-speed winds and lots of rain toward land. Dozens of hurricanes form every year and can cause massive damage to the areas they hit.

This radar image of a hurricane shows how large these storms can be. This storm is as big as an entire state.

Seasons of Daylight and Dark

Unlike the tropics where the seasons include monsoons and dry weather, the poles at either end of the earth experience seasons of daylight and dark. Because of the earth's 23.5° tilt, the sun's light passes across the ends of the earth. This means that at the North Pole the sun shines for six months. Then the sun sets and the North Pole is dark for six months.

As you move south from the North Pole, your days and nights become shorter than six months, but they can still be quite long. In Greenland, for example, it is dark for three months at a time. When the sun finally comes up, it shines for only a short time before disappearing again. Each day brings more sunshine until the sun stays up for three months. Then the cycle begins again.

At the North and South Poles, the sun never climbs high in the sky. Instead, for part of each year it circles around the horizon and never goes down. The photographer took this picture by placing a camera in one spot and taking 17 pictures without moving the film or camera. It shows the sun in 17 different places, all close to the horizon, in part of one day.

10:00 P.M.

11:00 P.M.

12:00 A.M.

1:00 A.M.

At the other end of the earth is the South Pole. When the North Pole is having six months of daylight, the South Pole has six months of darkness. Because they are at opposite ends of the planet, when one pole tilts toward the sun, the other pole is tilting away. If you are at the North Pole in summer or at the South Pole in winter, you don't follow the sun's path by looking high up in the sky and then back down again. You just turn your head in a circle.

This picture could have been taken in the middle of the night in the "Land of the Midnight Sun" near the North Pole.

5:00 A.M.

4:00 A.M.

3:00 A.M.

2:00 A.M.

If the seasons around the world didn't come and go as they do, and if the seasons weren't as predictable as they are, farmers and others who lived off the land would not have been able to survive and do so well. Their lives would have been like a guessing game, and it would have taken only a few wrong guesses to lose all crops or livestock.

You now know that not all seasons are spring, summer, fall, or winter. You also know a great deal about why we have seasons, and what the seasons in other parts of the world are like. You have learned how important knowledge of the seasons has been throughout history. What will you say now if someone asks you what season it is? Spring? Monsoon? Hurricane?

GLOSSARY

astronomer someone who studies the stars and planets

atmosphere the gases surrounding our planet, including oxygen

axis a real or imaginary straight center line in the middle of a spinning object

degree one unit of measurement in a circle

dormancy the period of time during which a living thing slows down its growth and rests for a while, such as over the winter

ellipse oval shape or path

hemisphere one-half of a sphere, or round object

hibernate to sleep or almost sleep for a period of time, such as over the winter

horizon the place where the sky and the land seem to meet

insulator a material that slows heat or cold from moving to another location

migrate to travel for a while to a distant location

predictable expected

revolution passing in a complete circle around another object

rotation turning around a center point

sowing planting seeds

spherical a shape that is round like a ball

INDEX